MIRANDA'S MONSTER

MIRANDA'S MONSTER

by GRISELDA GIFFORD
Illustrated by Julie Park

HODDER AND STOUGHTON
LONDON SYDNEY AUCKLAND TORONTO

To John with love

British Library Cataloguing in Publication Data
Gifford, Griselda
   Miranda's monster.
   I. Title   II. Park, Julie
823'.914[J]   PZ7

ISBN 0-340-41156-2

Text copyright © Griselda Gifford 1987
Illustrations copyright © Julie Park 1987

First published 1987

Published by Hodder and Stoughton Children's Books,
a division of Hodder and Stoughton Ltd,
Mill Road, Dunton Green, Sevenoaks, Kent TN13 2YJ

Printed in Belgium by Henri Proost et Cie, Turnhout

All rights reserved

Miranda watched the big yellow digger next door. It was making a hole so a house could be built.

She thought it looked like a huge hungry bird. All day it bent its neck to slurp up another load of earth in its metal mouth. It had been raining and the hole was filled with water. Miranda thought that Mud Monsters might live in the hole.

When evening came the digger was still. The pool was dark and there were strange shadows.

Miranda looked through the hole in the fence. She saw a large white thing floating on the pool. There was a funny cracking sound and the white thing fell apart.

"Mummy!" called a faint voice.
Miranda fetched her red boots and her torch.
She pushed through the gap in the fence. She sloshed into the mud and the water came to the top of her boots.
"Mummy! Mummy!" squeaked the voice.

Mummy!

The setting sun shone on the white thing in the water. Miranda saw that it was a huge egg! The shell was cracked in two, and something was crawling out of it. This something had huge eyes and a long blue nose like an elephant's trunk.

It flopped into the water and swam to the digger.

"Mummy!" it squeaked. It scrambled up to the digger on its two blue legs. There it stood, shivering.

"Mummy, I'm hungry!"

Miranda paddled out of the hole and scrambled up the side. Her boots had come off and floated in the pool. She was covered in mud, but she didn't mind. She had to rescue the poor baby Mud Monster.

"Mummy – feed me!" the baby Monster was saying to the digger.

Miranda oozed up to it on bare feet. She picked it up. "That's not your mummy!" she said.

The Mud Monster wriggled in her hands. Tears fell from its big eyes.

"I want Mummy!" it cried.

Miranda had to help it. "I'm your Mummy," she said.

The Mud Monster cuddled up to her. Its blue elephant trunk stroked her face.

"Mummy," it said. "Hungry."

Miranda took the Monster to her bedroom. She wrapped it in an old jumper because it was cold.

"Bath-time," called her mother.

Miranda put the Mud Monster in the pocket of her dressing-gown. She had to fold its long legs round its body. The Monster squealed a bit.

"Stop making that silly noise, Miranda," said Mum.

The Mud Monster jumped out of the bath. It was now the size of a rabbit!

Miranda hid the Monster in her room.

"Mummy!" called the Monster. "Hungry!"

"Just in time then," said Mum, as she brought in Miranda's cocoa and biscuits.

The Monster did not like biscuits . . .

"Ugh!"

But it did like leather. The Monster especially liked Miranda's school shoes. It was now the size of a cat!

"Come back!" cried Miranda, but it was too late. The Monster was on its way downstairs . . .

Miranda heard a crunchy sound and a loud belch.

Miranda ran downstairs after the Monster. She was afraid her mother would discover it.

"I'll have to hide you again," she said.

"Where's my handbag?" said Mum. "I left it here on the stairs. Miranda! Go to bed at once."

"Mummy, hungry!" squealed the Monster. It hopped out of Dad's boot, where Miranda had hidden it, and along the corridor towards the kitchen door.

"Of *course* you're not hungry, Miranda," said Mum. "I wonder if my handbag is in the kitchen."

"Of course, if you really are hungry you can have some milk out of the fridge," said Mum.

"No thank you," said Miranda.

The telephone rang in the living room, and Mum went to answer it.

Miranda pulled the Mud Monster from the fridge. It was in a terrible mess.

"Poor Mud Monster," said Miranda. "I wonder what I can give you to eat?"
 The Mud Monster soon found exactly what it wanted...
 It was now the size of a dog!

Miranda carried the Mud Monster upstairs to bed. It was very heavy indeed.

Miranda went to sleep, worrying about the Monster. She warmed it with her feet.

"Mummy!" cried the Monster in the night. "Hungry!"

Miranda put on the light. The Mud Monster was staring at her from the end of the bed. It had grown two big teeth.

She gave it a leather belt, which it ate in two huge gulps.

"Hungry," it said again, stroking her cheek with its trunk.

It was now the size of a sheep!

Miranda knew she could not keep her new pet. It was very sad, but she could never give it enough to eat.

"I'm not really your mummy," she said. "Come with me." She looped her dressing-gown cord round its neck and led it into the garden. Dawn was just breaking.

As they crossed the lawn the Monster scrunched up an old dog's lead. Within minutes it was the size of a lion!

Miranda and the Monster looked through the hole in the fence.

"Call Mummy loudly," said Miranda.

"MUMMY!" roared the Mud Monster. Now it was so big it had a very loud voice.

"Miranda!" called Mum from the bedroom window. "What on earth are you doing out there shouting at this time in the morning?"

"I'm looking for the Monster's mummy," said Miranda, but Mum had slammed the window shut.

From the middle of the pool came a glopping noise. The tip of a long blue trunk snaked out of the water.

Then a HUGE Mud Monster appeared. It was the size of an elephant.

The Mummy Monster ate Miranda's floating boots. Then it hopped to the fence on long blue legs.

"BABY!" it boomed, very loudly.

BABY!

Its long blue trunk wrapped round the baby Mud Monster and lifted it over the fence.

"Goodbye," called Miranda sadly.

There was a big splash. The Mud Monsters sank into the water. One large bubble came to the top of the pool.

Then there was just the yellow digger and silence.

Miranda's mother and father were very cross when they found Miranda's red boots and her school shoes had gone. "And there's a big hole in your slipper," said Mum.

"My briefcase has disappeared," said Dad.

"And I never found my handbag," said Mum.

They both looked at Miranda.

"Things don't just disappear," said Dad.

"They were eaten by a Mud Monster," Miranda said. They didn't believe her.

"Come and see the Monsters," said Miranda. Dad went back to bed, but Mum came with her.

"Look," said Miranda, pointing over the fence. Miranda's red boots came flying out of the pool.

"Mud Monsters only eat leather," Miranda explained. Mum looked into the pool and saw . . .

"Well I never!" she said.